This book is to be returned on or before
the last date stamped below.

1 7 APR 2002
− 4 OCT 2016

THE
VIETNAM
WAR

PAUL DOWSWELL

an imprint of Hodder Children's Books

© 2002 White-Thomson Publishing Ltd

Produced for Hodder Wayland by
White-Thomson Publishing Ltd
2/3 St Andrew's Place
Lewes
BN7 1UP

Series concept: Alex Woolf
Editor: Nicola Edwards
Designer: Derek Lee
Proofreader and Indexer: Sue Lightfoot
Consultant: Dr J. M. Bourne, Senior Lecturer in Modern
History, University of Birmingham
Map illustrator: Nick Hawken

Thanks to Hugh Nolan

Published in Great Britain in 2002 by Hodder Wayland,
a division of Hodder Children's Books

The right of Paul Dowswell to be identified as the author of
this work has been asserted by him in accordance with the
Copyright, Designs and Patents Act 1988. Map illustrations
by Nick Hawken.

British Library Cataloguing in Publication Data
Dowswell, Paul
  Vietnam War. - (The Cold War)
  1. Vietnamese Conflict, 1961-1975
  I. Title
  959.7'043

ISBN 0 7502 3394 X

Printed in Hong Kong by Wing King Tong

Hodder Children's Books
A division of Hodder Headline Limited
338 Euston Road, London NW1 3BH

Picture Acknowledgements: The publishers would like to thank the
following for giving permission to use their pictures:
Associated Press 47; Camera Press 16; Corbis cover (left), 20;
Eye Ubiquitous cover (centre), title page, 21, 26, 28, 36, 37, 41,
55, 58; Hulton Archive 39, 48; Pictorial Press Ltd 4; HWPL
17 (André Malvaux); Popperfoto cover (right), 7, 8, 12, 14, 15,
19, 29, 33, 43, 46, 52, 53, 54; Topham Picturepoint 5, 10, 22,
25, 27, 30, 34, 40, 44, 51, 56, 57.

Contents

CHAPTER ONE

A balcony on the Pacific: Vietnam up to 1946

WAR IN VIETNAM

The Vietnam War is fading into history. The 20-year struggle between South Vietnam and its American ally against the communist North Vietnamese, is remembered today through such films as *Platoon*, *Apocalypse Now* and *Rambo*. It is dimly recalled as an American tragedy, and it undoubtedly was. Over 47,000 American soldiers were killed in Vietnam, and more than 304,000 were wounded. For many young Americans drafted into the war, Vietnam would be a nightmare end to their adolescence. The dense tangled landscapes of Southeast Asia, with their strange place names – Da Nang, Khe San, the Plain of Jars – and the peasant people with their conical hats and chirping, birdlike language, must have seemed totally alien to a 19 year old from Ohio or Kansas. Such teenagers also had to contend with the prospect of imminent death from an enemy they rarely, if ever, glimpsed.

Along with personal tragedy, the war also brought national humiliation. While America was proving it was the world's most technologically advanced nation by putting men on the moon, it was also losing a war against a primitive, third world country, whose citizens lived lives that were medieval in their simplicity. When the war ended with a communist victory, Americans had to come to terms

▼ In one of the most tragic scenes of the movie *Platoon*, American Marine Sergeant Elias (played by Willem Dafoe), a father figure to his young troops, is hunted down by North Vietnamese soldiers.

with the fact that all the lives lost and billions of dollars spent had been wasted.

Although America was scarred by the war, the cost to Vietnam was much greater. Over three million Vietnamese lost their lives in the conflict, which was fought with great cruelty on both sides. The American airforce dropped more bombs on North Vietnam than it did on the Japanese during World War Two. In South Vietnam, American planes caused immense environmental damage, spraying chemical defoliants over vast tracts of jungle, intending to deprive North Vietnamese guerrilla forces of cover. In the day-to-day fighting, settlements from villages to cities were razed to the ground.

THE TV WAR

Journalists covering the fighting had greater access to the troops and action than at any conflict before or since. The brutal reality of the war was made plain to watching Americans every night on TV news bulletins. As villages burned to the ground and civilians were massacred, anti-war protests and civil unrest erupted throughout the United States.

▼ Vietnamese children, their flesh burning with napalm dropped by American planes, run screaming from the fighting. This photograph came to symbolize the dreadful effect of the war on Vietnam's civilian population.

A 'BALCONY ON THE PACIFIC'

The French called Vietnam their 'balcony on the Pacific'. It lies on the edge of Southeast Asia. China is to the north, Laos and Cambodia to the west, the South China Sea to the east. 1,025 miles (1,650 km) from top to bottom, this long, thin country can be split into four distinct areas. In the north is the densely populated Red River Delta, where Vietnam's capital Hanoi is located. In the South is the much bigger Mekong Delta, which is rich in agricultural land and home to Vietnam's second city, Saigon. Between these two deltas is a coastal plain where much of the population also live. Two-thirds of the country is taken up by the Annamese Cordillera – hills and mountains covered by dense forest. Vietnam's climate is generally hot and humid, with monsoon rains and frequent typhoons.

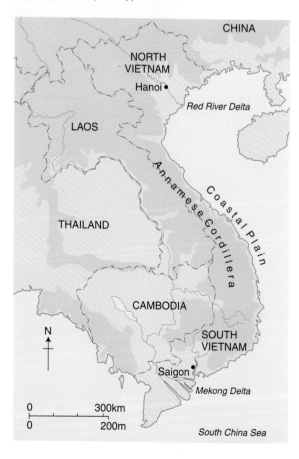

VIETNAM'S PAST

Before the war began, few people in the United States and Europe could point to Vietnam on a map. So how did this small, mountainous country come to assume so much importance to the West? The story starts over three thousand years ago, with the emergence of the Vietnamese people in what is now North Vietnam. China invaded this area, ruling it for a thousand years between 100BC and 900AD. The Vietnamese repeatedly rebelled against this foreign occupation, although their own culture became inextricably linked with China. The Vietnamese adopted Confucian philosophy, with its deep respect for the past, and the Buddhist religion.

The millennium-long occupation left the Vietnamese with a deep fear of Chinese domination. The arrival of Europeans in the sixteenth century led to further foreign interference, first by the Portuguese and then more effectively, by the French.

OCCUPIED BY THE FRENCH

Despite a long struggle against them, French troops finally conquered Vietnam in 1883. In 1893 the French lumped the country with Cambodia and Laos, and called this colonial territory French Indochina. The Vietnamese continued to rebel against this foreign occupation, and the 1930s saw strikes against the French and executions of rebels by the colonial authorities.

During World War Two (1939-1945) France was conquered by Germany, and ruled by a Nazi-approved fascist regime. Germany ceded French Indochina to its ally Japan, but the French continued to administer the country.

It was during this time that North Vietnam's great leader Ho Chi Minh came to prominence. Ho led resistance against the French and Japanese, and received arms and supplies from both the Chinese and United States. When the war ended, many Vietnamese, Ho included, expected both the defeated Japanese and the French to leave. But France was not prepared to give up her Far Eastern empire without a fight, and Vietnam was to face another thirty years of war before peace finally came.

During the 1920s and 30s Ho continued to travel around the world, visiting the Soviet Union and China, finally ending up in Bangkok, Thailand. Here he made contact with several rebel Vietnamese factions, which he united as the 'Vietminh', under his leadership. He returned to North Vietnam during the Second World War, after 30 years away, where he plotted for his country's independence. When the war ended in 1945 he made a speech in Hanoi before 100,000 people, declaring Vietnam to be an independent country.

"The oppressed the world over are wrestling back their independence. We should not lag behind. Under the Vietminh banner, let us valiantly march forward."

From then until his death in 1969, Ho led the North Vietnamese, single-mindedly set on freeing his country from foreign control, and reuniting North and South as one communist nation.

HO CHI MINH (1890-1969)

Ho Chi Minh (which means 'he who enlightens') was the leader of the North Vietnamese communists from 1945 until his death in 1969. A slight, spindly figure, he suffered from tuberculosis, malaria and dysentery, but was an extraordinarily resilient and charismatic man. Originally named Nguyen Tat Thanh, he was the son of a teacher. As a young man, he also taught briefly, before becoming a sailor and travelling the world. He settled in Paris after the First World War, where he came into contact with left-wing political groups. He was greatly inspired by the communist take-over of Russia, and became a founder member of the French Communist Party.

CHAPTER TWO

Playing dominoes? The First Indochina War 1946-1954

SHABBY TREATMENT

Like many European powers, France treated its colonies shabbily, and Vietnam was no exception. When the French arrived in Vietnam in the 1840s, 80% of the country could read – a figure that would have shamed any European nation. By the time they left only 20% of Vietnamese were literate. The fact that powerful Saigon gangsters were among the most vocal supporters of the French says much about the corrupt, exploitative regime they presided over.

WRONG PLACE, WRONG TIME

In the United States, which had become the most powerful nation on Earth following the end of the Second World War, there was little support for the French desire to return to their colony. But if ever a country was in the wrong place at the wrong time, it was Vietnam. In the post-war world, huge events were unfurling on the world stage that would have tragic consequences for this tiny country. The Second World War had ended in Europe in the spring of 1945. But almost as soon as peace settled on the continent, the victors began to quarrel. Both sides quickly developed a fierce distrust of each other. The worsening situation developed into 'The Cold War' – a series of diplomatic incidents and stand-offs that, narrowly at times, stopped short of out-and-out war between the major powers.

On one side of the political divide were the capitalist democracies of Britain, the United States and France. On the other was

▼ The first Cold War warriors. British Prime Minister Churchill, US President Truman and Soviet Generalissimo Stalin meet at the end of the Second World War. Allies against Nazi Germany, they soon fell out when their common enemy was defeated.

8

the Soviet Union. Having just lost 20 million of its citizens in an appallingly brutal war with Nazi Germany, this powerful communist regime was anxious to protect itself from another attack by hostile states. It was also keen to preserve and increase its power in the world.

If the North Vietnamese had been led by a simple, straightforward nationalist, perhaps the 30-year fight for independence would never have happened. But Ho Chi Minh and his fellow leaders were communists. Their natural allies were sympathetic communist regimes. As the '40s drew to a close another powerful communist regime joined the Soviet Union to support them.

THE 'DOMINO THEORY'

In 1949 communist forces in China, led by Mao ZeDong, managed to defeat the ruling nationalist government after a bitter 20-year struggle. The North Vietnamese immediately had a hugely powerful neighbour, sympathetic to their aims and politics. This was an instant worry to the Western nations. In the 1940s and for the next three decades, many Western capitalist governments, especially the United States, viewed communism as some kind of virus, and feared that this political ideology would spread to neighbouring nations. This was known as the 'domino theory', after the game in which dominoes are lined up on their side. When one is knocked down the rest in the line all fall in turn.

To counteract this, the United States followed a broad policy of 'containment'. This meant they would try to prevent, by military force if necessary or possible, the spread of communism from any communist country to a non-communist country.

AMERICAN FOREIGN POLICY AND VIETNAM

Right from the start America was suspicious of Ho Chi Minh and his communist regime, and automatically assumed that Ho's objectives in Vietnam were part of a wider communist conspiracy to take over the whole of Asia.

In 1950 a National Security Council report stated:

"the threat of communist aggression against Indochina is only one phase of anticipated communist plans to seize all of Southeast Asia."

But other American policy makers were not so sure. In the same year another State Department official, concerned by increasing American interest in Vietnam remarked:

"Whether the French like it or not, independence is coming to Indochina. Why therefore, do we tie ourselves to the tail of their battered kite?"

WAR IN KOREA

No sooner had the communists seized power in China than
an international catastrophe broke out on their doorstep.
Korea, a peninsula parallel with Japan, which also bordered
China, had a similar political situation to Vietnam. The north
of the country was controlled by communists, and the south
was controlled by a non-communist regime. War broke out
between them in 1950, and the United States and a United
Nations peace-keeping force rushed to defend the south. When
US forces swept north and advanced towards the Chinese
border, Chinese troops joined the war to defend the north. A
series of dramatic victories and defeats saw opposing forces
rampaging 700km from one end of the country to another,
before the hostile armies settled around the middle of the
country, roughly where the original division had been. An
armistice was signed in 1953, and an uneasy truce settled on
the country.

COLD WAR ATTITUDES

The United States feared a similar situation could occur in
Vietnam. Although they regarded France's possession of the
country with distaste, they supported the French with four

billion dollars of military aid. Initially, this was to show support for the French government against a strong communist opposition in France, but once China became communist, and the Korean War broke out, Vietnam became important in itself. Due to the Cold War attitudes that shaped American foreign policy, the North Vietnamese struggle against the colonial French was now seen as a communist conspiracy to grab the whole of Southeast Asia.

FRANCE TAKES ACTION

France had its own reasons for not letting go. During the Second World War it had been occupied and humiliated by Germany. Now the war was over, it wanted to regain some of its previous prestige and power. French troops began an active campaign against Ho's Vietminh forces, driving them from the northern capital Hanoi, and other cities such as the port of Haiphong, where a French navy bombardment killed 6,000 residents.

Ho's military commander, a former Hanoi law student named Vo Nguyen Giap, quickly discovered that when his Vietminh forces fought the French in conventional battles he invariably suffered heavy casualties. So he changed tactics, and began a campaign of guerrilla warfare. His troops set ambushes, planted mines, carried out hit and run raids and sniper attacks, and whittled away at the French forces, breaking both their morale and French public support for the war. In this way, the conflict dragged on for eight years.

Eventually, French generals decided on a ruse to draw the Vietminh forces out into the open. In March 1954, they set up a major armed camp in a remote valley in the north-west of the country named Dien Bien Phu. 16,500 French soldiers dug themselves in and waited for the Vietminh to attack.

A FRENCH PERSPECTIVE

An excerpt from French General Thomas Trapnall's report on the situation in Indochina in 1954:

"It is a savage conflict fought in a fantastic country in which the battle may be waged one day in waist-deep muddy rice paddies or later in an impenetrable mountainous jungle. The sun saps the vitality of friend and foe alike... It is a war with no immediate solution, a politico-military chess game in which the players sit thousands of miles distant – in Paris, Washington, Peking and Moscow..."

FRANCE DEFEATED

Attack the Vietminh did, but not in the way the French had imagined. Surrounding Dien Bien Phu was a ring of high hills. The Vietminh (together with thousands of Chinese volunteers), hauled large artillery up them, hiding their guns in caves, where they would be safe from air attack. French aircraft were further hindered by the constant mist that settled on the hills, making it extremely difficult to see targets on the ground.

In their fortified camp, the French ground troops were pulverized by incessant bombardment. Despite this, Dien Bien Phu was still well defended against all-out attack. Following heavy losses in frontal assaults, the Vietminh took to digging tunnels under the perimeter. During lulls in the shelling the exhausted French troops could hear the clattering of shovels as the enemy burrowed into their midst, occasionally bursting out of the ground in a desperate suicide attack.

After two months, the French surrendered. The battle of Dien Bien Phu had lost them the war, and they gave up their colony. 75,000 French soldiers died in fighting or from disease – a much greater figure than the American dead of the two decades to come. More significantly, both to the country and the final outcome of the war, 300,000 Vietnamese had died in this struggle for independence. They may have lacked the technology and economic

▼ Their faces showing terrible strain and exhaustion, French soldiers await another attack by Vietnamese troops at Dien Bien Phu. All around them are supplies dropped into the besieged camp by parachute.

power of the French, but the Vietnamese had a drive and determination that would consistently enable them to defeat forces far stronger than themselves.

THE GENEVA ACCORDS

The war ended with a conference in Geneva, Switzerland, and a settlement known as the Geneva Accords. In attendance were the Vietminh, now known as the Democratic Republic of Vietnam, the non-communist Vietnamese, France, China, the Soviet Union, United States and Britain.

The Vietminh assumed their victory over the French would give them control of the whole country, but it was not to be. Contrary to Western fears of a communist conspiracy plotting to take over the world, the Chinese and Russian representatives both urged the North Vietnamese to agree to a settlement that would be acceptable to the United States, France and Britain.

Ten weeks of wrangling produced an agreement. France would give up her former colony and Vietnam would be divided into the communist North and the non-communist South. There would be an election within two years to decide who would rule a united Vietnam. It all seemed quite simple. But then, nothing ever is…

DIVIDED VIETNAM 1954

Following the settlement reached at the Geneva Accords in 1954, Vietnam was temporarily divided into North and South, and a national election would then decide who ruled the country. The central area that marked the division between the two sides was called the Demilitarized Zone, or DMZ.

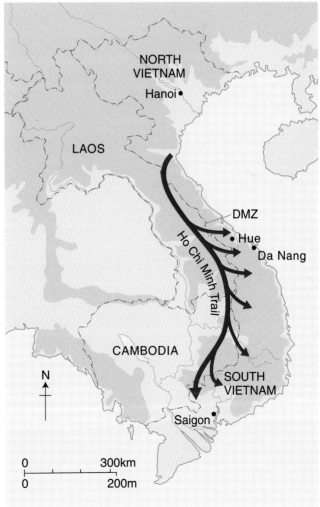

CHAPTER THREE

The onrushing tide: The Second Indochina War begins 1954-1963

COLD WAR POLITICS

Laid out, the events covered in this book have an awful inevitability about them. Looking back 50 years, it seems obvious that the shambolic South Vietnamese regime would never be able to resist the much more strongly motivated and better organised North. But perspective is always clearer from a distance.

By 1955, the last French troops had left Vietnam. America rushed to fill their place – not as an occupying colonial power, but as a friendly 'big brother' – intent on protecting the South from communism. The fate of Vietnam was irrevocably bound up with the Cold War politics of the 1950s. Without the Cold War, America would never have backed the incompetent South Vietnamese government so strongly.

US FEAR OF COMMUNISM

In the years following the Second World War, and especially in the 1950s, America's fear of the political philosophy of communism, and countries that had adopted this political system, had intensified – especially when the Soviet Union began to build nuclear weapons to rival America's. Within the United States a senator named Joseph McCarthy had convinced large numbers of Americans that their country was seething with communist spies. McCarthy instigated a series of 'witch hunts' intent on denouncing anyone in public life who had left-wing sympathies. A blinkered mindset developed where the world was divided into communist and 'free' nations.

As the Cold War grew colder, Vietnam settled into its post-Geneva circumstances. In the North Ho Chi Minh was the undisputed leader of the Communist government. In the South the head of state Bao Dai appointed Ngo Dinh Diem as Prime Minister.

DIEM LEADS SOUTH VIETNAM

Diem, as he was generally known, had taken on an immensely difficult job. He had no effective armed forces, no police force, no civil service and a weak economy, weakened even further by the migration of 900,000 Vietnamese from the north who were fleeing the communist regime there. On top of this, he had many enemies. Within the South, there was still strong support for Ho, especially in the countryside. Powerful, armed religious groups called the Cao Dai and Hoa Hao, and gangster private armies also threatened his regime. On top of this, Diem was a Catholic in a predominantly Buddhist society.

A situation like this demanded a leader capable of uniting these varying factions. But Diem had no such qualities. He took decisive, violent action against both the religious groups and gangsters, but in such a clumsy way that many innocent people were killed, stirring up more opposition against him. Worst of all, having come to government with little support, he refused to share power with other political groups. Instead, he placed members of his own family in important political positions. His brother Ngo Dinh Nhu, for example, was head of the secret police. As well as being Diem's confidant and closest advisor, Nhu was also a drug addict.

NGO DINH DIEM (1901-1963)

Diem was a haughty, solemn man. American journalist Stanley Karnow described him as *"a rotund little figure whose feet barely touched the floor when he sat on the elegant chairs… of the palace. He looked as fragile as porcelain, with delicate features and ivory skin, but his eyes projected a fanatical faith in his crusade."*

In 1961, US Vice-president Lyndon Johnson described him as *"… the Churchill of the decade… in the vanguard of those leaders who stand for freedom."* When Stanley Karnow asked Johnson if he had meant what he said, the Vice-president replied *"****, Diem's the only boy we got out there."*

US RESERVATIONS

American politicians had serious reservations about Diem, but he was staunchly anti-communist, and no other alternative was immediately apparent. Prompted by American advisors, Diem was encouraged to forget about the planned elections agreed in the Geneva Accords, which he would almost certainly have lost. Instead, with American help, he was to set about forming a separate independent nation in South Vietnam. Curiously, in the North, Ho and his regime accepted this clear breach of the Geneva treaty, and were encouraged to do so by their Soviet and Chinese allies.

Ho hoped that the people in the South would rise up against Diem's regime, and topple him themselves. The Chinese and Soviet Union were keen to avoid having America involve itself in a major war in Vietnam, which they knew would happen if the North tried to take over the South.

▲ North Vietnamese guerrilla forces push supplies down the Ho Chi Minh Trail. The North's 'low-tech' approach to the war was ultimately more effective than America's reliance on high technology weapons and transport.

'DENOUNCE A COMMUNIST'

But with a characteristic lack of political cunning, Diem thought he could strengthen his position by attacking Ho's supporters in the South. He instigated a 'Denounce a communist' campaign which in turn led the pro-communists in South Vietnam to organise into fighting groups to defend themselves. These groups became known by their enemies as the 'Vietcong' – a term that would remain in use throughout the war.

By 1957 fighting between communist rebels and South Vietnam's ARVN troops (Army of the Republic of Vietnam) had resulted in over 2,000 deaths, and the arrest of over 65,000 'communist suspects'. The communists in turn retaliated by assassinating local government officials, and carrying out guerrilla skirmishes against the ARVN.

As fighting continued, Ho's regime adopted a more hands-on policy. Instead of leaving their friends in the South to their own devices, North Vietnam now began to actively supply them with both armed support and equipment. A ramshackle, but effective supply route, dubbed the Ho Chi Minh trail (see pages 13 and 23), was set up to do this. As well as passing from North to South Vietnam, the trail also intruded into neighbouring Laos and Cambodia.

By the end of 1957, the conflict in the South had intensified into civil war. Diem reacted by ordering the formation of 'Agrovilles' – fortified villages away from communist controlled areas, where peasants were forcibly moved from their homes to isolate and protect them from communist rebels. Such a clumsy policy made Diem even more unpopular. At the end of 1960, the communists and other groups opposed to Diem formed a broad opposition, which they called the National Liberation Front.

JOHN F. KENNEDY (1917-1963)

Following on from Dwight Eisenhower's drab presidency, John F. Kennedy and his beautiful wife Jackie seemed impossibly glamorous. Kennedy was the son of Joseph Kennedy, a multi-millionaire businessman who had been ambassador to Britain during the Second World War. Although his presidential opponent Richard Nixon had taunted him as being *"soft on communism"*, Kennedy came to power convinced that America had a duty to stop what he described as *"the onrushing tide of communism"* from engulfing all Asia.

▼ America's most glamorous couple, John and Jackie Kennedy (left and centre), greet guests at a White House social event. Just behind Jackie stands Vice-president Lyndon Johnson.

NEW PRESIDENT, OLD ANXIETIES

In the United States anxiety over Vietnam was growing more acute. Newly-elected President John F. Kennedy took the same view as his predecessor, Dwight Eisenhower. If Diem was defeated, the communists would take over. According to the 'domino theory' (see page 9), communism would then spread like a plague to neighbouring Burma, India and then even Africa. With so much at stake, Kennedy decided that Diem must be supported at all costs.

MORE US INVOLVEMENT

American intervention increased. Military advisors began to train the ARVN, and the American intelligence service, the CIA, organised other anti-communist groups within the South. Diem's unpopular Agroville policy was further developed and 3,700 'Strategic Hamlets' of fortified villages were set up in the countryside. The intention here again was to isolate peasants from anti-government forces, and provide strongpoints inside the natural rebels' territory of the countryside. But no matter how much assistance the US provided, what they could not buy for Diem was the support of the Vietnamese people.

The situation deteriorated. In 1963, the war against communist forces in the South was going so badly that 2,600 Strategic Hamlets had been destroyed. But curiously, it was not the communists that led to Diem's downfall, but the Buddhists. Among Diem's powerful relatives was his brother, the Roman Catholic Archbishop Ngo Dihn Thuc. Despite the fact that Buddhism was the main religion in Vietnam, Thuc had forbidden the display of Buddhist flags during a Buddhist holiday. This characteristic family arrogance led to demonstrations. Government troops were called out, and shot several Buddhist monks dead. Temples were raided and martial law declared.

BLACK AND WHITE PERSPECTIVE

Both sides in the Vietnam War liked to depict the other as monstrous. Such deep-set attitudes discouraged any real understanding between the enemies:

Ho Chi Minh told his people that victory by the North would bring "… an era of right and justice… in the struggle of civilisation against barbarism."

President Kennedy described capitalist America's conflict against communism as "a struggle for supremacy between two conflicting ideologies: freedom under God versus ruthless, godless tyranny."

BUDDHIST PROTESTS

So outraged were Buddhists that some took to burning themselves to death in the street. Photographs of these extraordinary acts immediately spread around the world. Diem's sister-in-law Madame Nhu's callous dismissal of the protests as "Buddhist barbecues" spoke volumes about the moral fabric of Diem's family. "Let them burn," she said "and we shall clap our hands."

The quarrel with the Buddhists was

the final straw. When US government officials in Vietnam were informed of an army plot to remove Diem, they said nothing. On 1st November 1963, ARVN troops ousted Diem, and executed him and his brother Nhu. Although the American government were shocked by the killings, they could at least hope for a leader who might be more effective.

But more shocks were in store. On 22nd November, President Kennedy was shot dead in Dallas. He was a strong supporter of American involvement in Vietnam. His successor, Vice- president Lyndon Baines Johnson was not so sure.

▼ As Saigon residents look on with almost nonchalant curiosity, another Buddhist monk burns himself to death in protest against religious discrimination in South Vietnam. Diem's feud against the Buddhists led directly to his deposition and assassination.

CHAPTER FOUR

Just like the five o'clock news: The United States and full-scale war 1964-1967

▲ President Lyndon Johnson's hopes for great social reforms in America were scuppered by the social strife and economic cost of the war in Vietnam.

JOHNSON'S DILEMMA

History will remember President Lyndon Johnson as the man who committed the United States to war in Vietnam. But history can be very unfair. Johnson's great vision when he came to power was, not to entangle America in a major foreign war, but a strong desire to make America a better, fairer place.

Like all American presidents in office during the course of the Vietnam War, Johnson's problem lay in the Cold War thinking of the era. The South Vietnamese were forever teetering on the brink of defeat, but America could not let them fall. Johnson's strategy was to continue to support the South in a way that would still enable him to push through his 'Great Society' policies (see page 21), and minimise public opposition to the war. But he was never able to do this.

When Johnson came to power, following the assassination of President Kennedy in November 1963, the situation in Vietnam was as bad as ever. Although the South had more troops at their command, and were better supplied, they were still losing out to the rebels, who now controlled over a third of South Vietnam. The rebels were now so confident they were attacking Southern forces directly, rather than engaging in guerrilla warfare. Johnson's military advisors predicted an imminent collapse, and the president felt he had no option but to prop up the South with yet more American aid.

THE GULF OF TONKIN RESOLUTION

Johnson needed an excuse to enable him to do this, so he could sell the increased expense and likely loss of American lives to the American people. In August 1964 North Vietnamese patrol boats fired on American navy ships in the Gulf of Tonkin, off the coast of North Vietnam. The American ships were providing cover for South Vietnamese commando raids, so the North Vietnamese had every reason to think they were a legitimate target. But Johnson was able to present the attack to Congress (the American Government) as an example of North Vietnamese aggression, and evidence of the North's intention to wage war against the United States. Congress supported him, passing 'The Gulf of Tonkin Resolution' which gave the US president power to make military decisions without consulting Congress.

Greater American involvement would mean greater American casualties, which would automatically bring greater opposition to the war from the American people. To minimise this, Johnson decided that the best way to wage war would be to use the US airforce, which was almost certainly the most powerful and sophisticated fighting machine on the planet. Johnson hoped that US bombers would quickly destroy the North's ability to wage war, with minimal loss of American lives. This was the intention of 'Operation Rolling Thunder', which commenced in March 1965.

Johnson called his dream 'The Great Society'. He wanted his government to bring in laws and policies to discourage racial prejudice, lessen poverty, and improve the healthcare and education available to the poorest Americans.

"In your time we have the opportunity to move not only toward the rich society and the powerful society, but upward to the Great Society."

PRESIDENT LYNDON JOHNSON, IN A SPEECH TO UNIVERSITY OF MICHIGAN STUDENTS, 1964

"The Great Society has been shot down on the battlefield of Vietnam."

CIVIL RIGHTS CAMPAIGNER MARTIN LUTHER KING, 1967

▼ US Navy personnel prepare to launch an F-4 Phantom bomber from the deck of USS *Midway*, stationed near the North Vietnamese mainland. American airpower was effective, but never crucial to the outcome of the war.

'OPERATION ROLLING THUNDER'

At the time, 'Operation Rolling Thunder' was the most massive bombing campaign in history. American planes disgorged thousands of tons of bombs, destroying the factories, roads, bridges and supplies of North Vietnam. Perhaps $340 million worth of damage was caused, and thousands of Vietnamese were killed. US airforce officer Curtis E. LeMay summed up American intention and attitude perfectly when he said "They've got to draw in their horns and stop their aggression, or we're going to bomb them back into the Stone Age."

But LeMay was missing the point. The people of Vietnam were not primitive, but their country was one of the most low-tech nations on Earth. Such a bombardment would have caused immense damage to an industrialized nation, but the North Vietnamese did not rely on technology. They were essentially an agricultural society, with the most rudimentary transport systems and industry. (Even today the main railway line between North and South Vietnam is still a single track.) Roads, railways and factories were quickly rebuilt, and aid from China and the Soviet Union made up for the losses of arms and other supplies.

▼ The first American combat soldiers spill out of landing craft on the beaches of Da Nang in March 1965. Within four years there would be over half a million US troops in Vietnam.

THE HO CHI MINH TRAIL

Nothing illustrated the low-tech/high-determination philosophy of the North Vietnamese better than the Ho Chi Minh trail. Stretching from the North into the South, this makeshift route was the main conduit for North Vietnamese soldiers, and arms and provisions for Southern rebels throughout the war (see page 13). It took between two and six months to travel down it. Sometimes troops and equipment were ferried by lorry, more often than not they walked or pushed supplies on bicycles (see page 16). Up to one in five who set out to reach South Vietnam died en route, from exhaustion, illness and the frequent air attacks.

American planes did not have everything their own way. During the course of the war, North Vietnamese fighter planes, missiles and anti-aircraft guns were increasingly effective, and the greatest number of American prisoners of war during the conflict would be aircrew.

"The Americans thought the more bombs they dropped, the quicker we would fall to our knees and surrender. But the bombs heightened rather than dampened our spirit."

NORTH VIETNAMESE DOCTOR, TON THAT TUNG

COMBAT TROOPS GO IN

During the 1964 election, Johnson had promised America: "We are not about to send American boys nine or ten thousand miles away from home to do what Asian boys ought to be doing for themselves." But much against his own wishes, that is exactly what he did.

Increased air combat meant that American bases had to be built in Vietnam. The commander in chief General Westmoreland was concerned that the South Vietnamese army was not up to the task of defending these bases, and requested that American soldiers should do the job. The first American combat troops landed in Da Nang in March 1965. Other troops from America's allies were also sent to support the ailing South Vietnamese. Among other nations 8,000 Australian and 60,000 South Korean troops fought there.

23

AMERICA'S INVOLVEMENT INCREASES

American generals were convinced that the South Vietnamese army would not win the war, and were impatient to send their own men to fight the communists. Said Earle Wheeler, the chairman of the Joint Chiefs of Staff, "You must carry the fight to the enemy. No one ever won a battle sitting on his ass."

Wheeler's opinion won the day with good reason. The ARVN forces had always been reluctant to fight, and as American involvement increased, many South Vietnamese felt that American soldiers could do their fighting for them. Every year one third of the ARVN deserted.

'SEARCH AND DESTROY'

At the end of 1964 there were 23,000 American soldiers in Vietnam. Barely three years later there were 535,000. Taking the offensive General Westmoreland pursued a strategy called 'Search and Destroy'. Intending to locate and eradicate rebel groups in the South, he used all the high technology weapons at his disposal. Helicopters ferried troops out to remote countryside landing zones near to where enemy forces were reported to operate. The troops dropped there kept in constant radio touch with their headquarters. Officers could call in air strikes within minutes, from off-shore carriers with ground support aircraft in constant readiness to aid troops in the field.

COMBAT EXPERIENCE

Having grown used to watching the war on television, many new soldiers in Vietnam found the experience of being there quite unreal.

*"I heard some Skyhawks (US jet planes) coming in dropping bombs… It was just like the five o'clock news back home. There were some gunships and a 34 (US helicopter) comes in and all of a sudden it bursts into flames and drops straight out of the sky… All of a sudden this guy comes running up… He says 'Saddle up, we're going to help…' I thought 'Holy ****! Here I am a spectator, now I'm going to be in the middle of this thing.' I was scared beyond description."*

LANCE CORPORAL GARY CONNOR

AGENT ORANGE

These planes could incinerate enemy troops with napalm – a ferocious, petrol-based burning fluid – or lacerate them with machine guns that could fire over a hundred rounds a second. American planes also began to spray vast tracts of Vietnam (3.6 million acres in all) with herbicides such as Agent Orange, which destroyed the dense rainforest communist guerrillas used for cover and food.

▲ Dense emerald-green forest is turned to a dusty wasteland to make a landing zone for American helicopters. These machines could transport troops into battle and evacuate wounded men very speedily, but they were all too easy to shoot down.

Diem's assassination in November 1963 did not bring political stability to South Vietnam. Instead a succession of four different heads of state followed in quick succession. In February 1965 Air Marshall Nguyen Cao Ky became leader. He in turn was succeeded by Nguyen Van Thieu in September 1967, who stayed in power until the collapse of the South in 1975.

Thieu had close links with the West. A Catholic who had been an officer in the French colonial army, he also received military training in the United States. The government he headed was described as "absolutely the bottom of the barrel" by William Bundy, one of President Johnson's advisors. Thieu was just as corrupt as many other South Vietnamese officials, and took millions of dollars of gold with him when he fled from Vietnam in 1975.

A PYRRHIC VICTORY

At first it seemed like Westmoreland's campaign would succeed. Communist casualties between 1965 and 1967 numbered nearly 200,000, with American losses running at a highly favourable 13,500. It looked like America's reliance on their technological superiority was both winning the war and keeping their own casualties low. But ultimately, Westmoreland's strategy failed for the same reasons the bombing campaign had. Whenever American soldiers cleared an area of rebel forces they would be back within months.

▲ As their transport helicopter returns to base, soldiers of the US 73rd Airborne Division begin a nerve-wracking patrol in Vietcong territory.

The communist soldiers who fought in the South had two great advantages over their enemies. Much of the time they had the support of the peasants in the areas they operated in, and could melt into anonymity whenever hostile troops approached. They could also decide when and where to attack. Throughout the war nine out of ten encounters between communist and American troops were set up by the communists. The Americans and South Vietnamese merely looked for the enemy, more often than not only finding them when they were attacked.

THE DRAFT

The American Government needed to increase the size of the army, to fight in Vietnam. From 1965, male American teenagers over 18 were called up to serve in the armed forces for two years, in a procedure known as 'the Draft.' Young people at college, who were mainly middle-class, were allowed to avoid the Draft to finish their education, so most of those called up were from the poorer sections of American society.

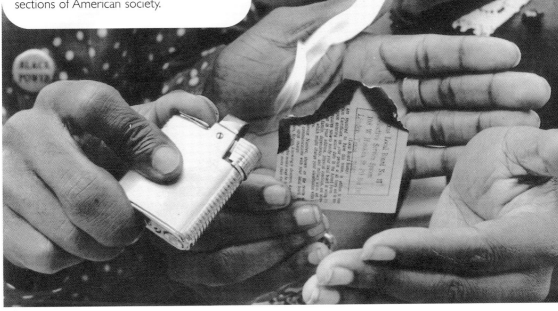

▼ The 'Draft' – the compulsory enlistment of American males aged over 18 into the armed forces – was instantly unpopular. Here, black American males burn their draft cards for press photographers.

CHAPTER FIVE

Dead, but too dumb to lie down? Tet and afterwards 1968

KHE SANH

As 1967 turned to 1968 America was in for a massive shock. The year started badly with attacks on isolated American bases. Worst hit was Khe Sanh, a Marine camp near the border with the North, which was besieged for several months. Khe Sanh took on a significance way beyond its importance, and became a symbol of America's refusal to be driven out of Vietnam.

General Westmoreland was so determined that the base would not fall that he airlifted in 6,000 troops and had B-52 bombers drop 100,000 tons of bombs on five square miles around the base to try to destroy the invisible enemy in the surrounding jungle. This was the most intense aerial bombardment in the history of warfare.

President Johnson became obsessed with the camp too. In a basement room in the White House, staff had constructed a sand-table model of the siege. At night Johnson would pace around in his dressing gown, reading the latest battle reports from the base. Yet, in one of the war's great ironies, as soon as Khe Sanh ceased to be a communist target, it was dismantled.

▼ The American stronghold at Khe Sanh in early 1968. Safe inside the perimeter, American troops consume their rations among the ugly debris of the camp.

THE TET OFFENSIVE

There was more to come. On the night of 30th January, 1968, North Vietnamese forces launched a major strike against the South, known as the Tet Offensive. 84,000 troops from both the regular army and Vietcong forces were involved.

The day was well chosen. Named after the national holiday in Vietnam celebrating the start of the Chinese lunar new year, the South was caught off guard by the attack. During the Tet celebrations it was customary to set off firecrackers and other fireworks. In Saigon after midnight, residents recalled hearing the usual celebratory fireworks, then realising that many of the bangs they heard were actually gunshots and exploding mortar shells. Thirty-six major cities and towns in South Vietnam were targeted, as the North shifted its military activities from the countryside to South Vietnam's urban centres.

In Saigon communist commandos destroyed the radio station, and attacked high profile targets such as the presidential palace, the South Vietnamese army general headquarters and the airport. Most alarmingly of all, for Americans at least, the United States Embassy was assaulted. A commando unit of 19 men broke into the embassy grounds and held out for several hours. One or two even managed to enter the embassy itself before they were killed. The American ambassador Ellsworth Bunker was asleep in his home nearby, but the night-duty officer felt he had to lock himself in the embassy code room to escape the attackers.

▲ High above Vietnam a giant American B-52 bomber spews out its high explosive cargo. No country on Earth has been more heavily bombed than Vietnam.

VO NGUYEN GIAP (1911-)

The architect of the Tet Offensive was Ho Chi Minh's right hand man, General Giap. A tiny, elf-like figure, Giap was North Vietnam's Vice-premier and Minister of Defence. Over 30 years he transformed the Vietminh guerrillas into a national fighting force capable of defeating both the French and American armies. Giap was blessed with soldiers willing to make great sacrifices to free their homeland, and he described his overall strategy thus: "Another twenty years, even a hundred years, as long as it took to win, regardless of cost."

▲ Among the ruins of their city, citizens of Hue attempt a return to normal life in March 1968. One of the main targets for the North in the Tet Offensive, the fighting in Hue created 100,000 refugees.

HUE

Outside of Saigon, the most significant attack came in the ancient city of Hue, close to the North Vietnamese border. Here 7,500 communist troops seized control of parts of the city for three weeks. During the occupation they behaved with great brutality. Up to 5,000 government officials, and other citizens who had links with the Americans and South Vietnamese regime, were executed. In the fighting to regain control of Hue, the city was destroyed, and 100,000 of its citizens became refugees. Altogether the offensive was to create a million refugees.

In some ways Tet was a disaster for the North. Over 30,000 North Vietnamese and Vietcong soldiers died during the offensive. All of the territory they seized was lost by the summer. The Vietcong would never be as strong again. Losses inflicted on the Americans and the South Vietnamese amounted to a mere 3,400 – barely 10% of their own.

The communists had also hoped that, given a little help, the citizens of South Vietnam would rise up against the regime there. But this never happened. Whether through fear, dislike or simply indifference, most South Vietnamese civilians neither supported nor joined the attacking soldiers in their midst.

STALEMATE?

But Tet had an impact way beyond the simple statistics of soldiers killed and land captured. It is best summed up by a bewildered remark by famous American television journalist Walter Cronkite: "What the hell is going on? I thought we were winning the war!" Although this comment was never broadcast, Cronkite went on to tell his television audience he was convinced that "the bloody experience of Vietnam is to end in stalemate."

General Westmoreland was certain in his own mind that the Tet Offensive was a communist defeat. But in reality Tet proved that the United States was not winning. Even with all its technology and half a million troops, they could not eradicate the forces set against them. Tet was the turning point of the war – the moment when many government officials realized they could not win. The billions of dollars spent on propping up the South had still left it weak and open to defeat. The so-called 'Pacification' programmes where US and ARVN troops had attempted to destroy communist forces had failed.

IMPACT OF TET

Journalist Michael Herr describes the impact of the Tet Offensive in his classic account of the war *Dispatches*: "*We took a huge collective nervous breakdown… every American in Vietnam got a taste. Vietnam was a dark room full of heavy objects, the VC were everywhere all at once like spider cancer, and instead of losing the war in little pieces over the years we lost it fast in under a week. After that,… we were dead but too dumb to lie down.*"

"*Until Tet they (the Americans) thought they could win the war, but now they knew they could not.*"

NORTH VIETNAM'S MILITARY COMMANDER GENERAL GIAP

PROTESTS BEGIN

The Tet offensive brought a major turnaround in American policy. Until Tet, General Westmoreland had had each demand for more troops granted. Now, his requests fell on sceptical ears.

As Johnson sat in the presidential office, protesters gathered at the railings outside the White House. Their chants of "Hey, Hey, LBJ, How many kids have you killed today?" drifted across the lawn. These taunts stirred a deep anger in him, and he would curse them bitterly. But Tet had left the President and his policy advisors in a terrible quandary. If more men, more money and more equipment was not going to win the war in Vietnam, what on earth was?

JOHNSON'S ANNOUNCEMENT

On 31st March, 1968, as his term in office neared its end, Johnson shocked his supporters by announcing he would not stand for re-election as president. He had prevented the South falling to communism and had managed to avoid an escalation in the war that could have brought America into direct conflict with communist China, or the Soviet Union, and now there was nowhere else to go.

AMERICAN TROOP NUMBERS IN VIETNAM

1960	900
1962	11,000
1965	(June) 50,000
1965	(December) 180,000
1967	389,000
1969	540,000
1970	335,000
1971	160,000
1973	160

PROTESTS CONTINUE

As American involvement in Vietnam deepened, all American presidents had to contend with noisy anti-war protests. Many protesters were students, or part of the hippy 'counter-culture' – an anti-authoritarian movement in American society which claimed to reject materialism, and enthusiastically embraced liberal experimentation with drugs and sex in a way that shocked older generations.

The anti-war demonstrations, which reached a peak in November 1969, with a march by 500,000 people in Washington, sent a message to both sides in the conflict. They were a warning to the government that they could only push the war so far, and that massive casualties would not be acceptable to the American people. They also let the North Vietnamese know that their American enemies did not have unconditional support at home.

Many other Americans though, supported their government's policy in Vietnam. The demonstrations stirred deep resentment among more conservative Americans.

▼ Waving a variety of flags, including that of communist North Vietnam, demonstrators in New York march in protest against America's involvement in the Vietnam War.

CHAPTER SIX

Peace with honour 1968-1970

'THE WILL TO WIN'

Republican presidential candidate Richard M. Nixon offered the American people an alternative to Johnson's Vietnam policy, and it won him the 1968 election. Nixon set out his policy in an article he wrote for the right-wing magazine Reader's Digest in 1964. Like many Americans he believed that a communist victory there would be a catastrophe. His solution was to make full use of American military might. He wrote: "All that is needed… is the will to win – and the courage to use our power."

Nixon won the 1968 presidential election because his policies for Vietnam had the most broadly-based appeal. Although many Americans opposed the war, many more felt that American troops should be fighting the communists there. Nixon, in a snide reference to the noisy demonstrations against

▼ Nixon on the campaign trail during the 1968 election. A familiar figure to Americans, thanks to his four year spell as Eisenhower's Vice-president, Nixon promised both to save America's dignity and end the war.

the war, referred to pro-war Americans as 'the silent majority'. During the election campaign he had promised voters that he would "end the war and win the peace".

'VIETNAMIZATION'

Nixon's vision, encapsulated in a handy sound bite, was "peace with honour". His intention was to push forward a policy Johnson had begun, that of 'Vietnamization'. South Vietnam would be offered American training and military equipment to build up their army to the point where they would be able to fight their communist opponents on their own. While they were doing this, American soldiers would remain in Vietnam, although their numbers would be gradually reduced.

RICHARD NIXON (1913-1994)

Richard Nixon had tasted power before. Between 1953 and 1960 he was Vice-president of the United States. He was a man who polarised opinion. Some admired his tough anti-communist stance. Others thought him a cynical, underhand opportunist, and nicknamed him 'Tricky Dicky'. Certainly, he had taken full advantage of the political hysteria the Cold War generated. He had been a prominent supporter of Joseph McCarthy, and his communist witch hunts. He once confided to a friend *"If you can't lie, you'll never go anywhere"*. Perhaps it was no great surprise that his presidential career would end in resignation and disgrace following the Watergate scandal.

DEFENDING THE 'FREE WORLD'

Once South Vietnam could fend for itself, America could withdraw without the disgrace of defeat. Like most American politicians at the time, Nixon felt it was hugely important for the United States to maintain its credibility as the champion of the 'free world'. Once committed to defending a nation against communism it could not be seen to fail or back down. To do so, ran the Cold War thinking of the day, would be to invite the Soviet Union or China to extend their communist tentacles to other countries, and take over even more of the world.

Once in power Nixon was determined to use all of America's military strength to achieve his aims. One of his first and most important appointments was that of Henry Kissinger as US National Security Advisor. Between them the two men would plot the course of American policy in Vietnam.

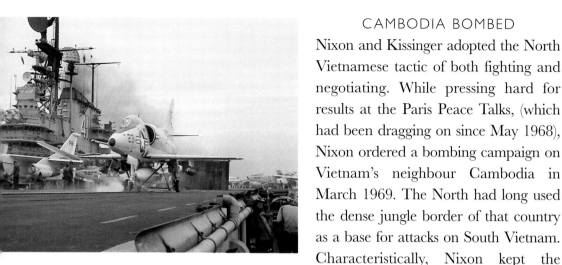

▲ America hoped that her airforce, arguably the most sophisticated fighting force in the world, would be able to wreak terrible havoc on the North Vietnamese, whilst keeping American casualties to an acceptable level.

CAMBODIA BOMBED

Nixon and Kissinger adopted the North Vietnamese tactic of both fighting and negotiating. While pressing hard for results at the Paris Peace Talks, (which had been dragging on since May 1968), Nixon ordered a bombing campaign on Vietnam's neighbour Cambodia in March 1969. The North had long used the dense jungle border of that country as a base for attacks on South Vietnam. Characteristically, Nixon kept the bombing secret from the American people. With some justification, he reasoned that the anti-war demonstrations this would provoke would encourage the communists to think that Nixon's own countrymen did not support him.

THE 'MADMAN THEORY'

Nixon also played up his anti-communist reputation, by threatening the North with "measures of great consequence and force" if they refused to negotiate with him. This was a thinly-veiled reference to America's huge nuclear missile arsenal. Nixon never intended to actually use these enormously destructive weapons, but confided to a presidential aide: "I call it the Madman theory... I want the North Vietnamese to believe I'll do anything to stop the war. We'll slip the word to them that 'for God's sake, you know Nixon is obsessed about communists. We can't restrain him when he's angry – and he has his hand on the nuclear button' – and Ho Chi Minh himself will be in Paris in two days begging for peace."

Nixon and his new government did have some grounds for optimism in early

HENRY KISSINGER (1923-)

Kissinger was a Jewish refugee from Nazi Germany. A brilliant, intensely ambitious academic, who spoke with a deep, guttural German accent, he would prove to be as ruthless and cunning as his boss.

In 1973 Nixon appointed him Secretary of State, a post he continued to hold under President Ford. He explained his attitude to international politics with these words: *"The superpowers often behave like two heavily-armed blind men feeling their way around a room, each believing himself in mortal peril from the other, whom he assumes to have perfect vision... Of course, even two blind men can do enormous damage to each other, not to speak of the room."*

1969. Although American military pride had taken a severe pounding during the Tet Offensive (see pages 29 to 32), and the people of the United States were divided over their support for the war, things weren't as bad as they seemed. Tet was, after all, a communist defeat. The North had played their best shot, and when the dust settled the South Vietnamese regime and their American allies were still there.

COLD WAR POLITICS

Furthermore, there were huge shifting currents in world politics, and Nixon was keen to take advantage of them. China and the Soviet Union may have both been communist regimes but, as with capitalist countries, they had significant political differences. During the 1960s relations between them grew frostier, and a border dispute in 1969 actually resulted in fighting between Soviet and Chinese troops. This increased hostility made both the Soviet Union and China feel they should seek better relations with the United States.

Throughout the Vietnam War the Soviet Union had been North Vietnam's staunchest supporter, but now the Soviets were losing enthusiasm. Originally, with classic Cold War logic, the Soviets had supported the North because it was fighting against America. They had sent a great deal of aid they could ill-afford. But as the war dragged on, Soviet politicians felt the goods they were sending to Vietnam would be better used to benefit their own country. They were as keen as the United States for the war to end. But like the United States, they did not want to be seen to abandon an ally, and appear to be weak to their Cold War enemies.

▼ These men, cruelly bound and blindfolded as they awaited interrogation by US forces, were suspected of being communist guerrillas.

LE DUAN TAKES OVER

Despite Nixon's threats, Ho Chi Minh did not rush to Paris to beg for peace. Even if he'd had the mind to, he would have been too ill. His health began to fail in early 1969. He worked until August of that year and then died, aged 79, on 2nd September. Ho's death inspired hopes in America that the North may take a softer line, but his successor Le Duan was made of the same stern stuff. The North still had one clear objective – the unification of Vietnam under their communist regime, and they were determined to see this through. All the American threats of bombing, and pressure to compromise brought by the Soviet Union, could not shift them.

FLAWS IN 'VIETNAMIZATION'

Meanwhile, 'Vietnamization' was proving difficult to implement. Nixon had spelled out the policy to President Thieu in June 1969. Like most other South Vietnamese politicians, he was greatly suspicious, seeing it as an excuse for an American withdrawal from the war. Even if Thieu had been enthusiastic, the policy still had a fatal flaw. The problem was the South Vietnamese army. Most of its officers were an alarming combination of corrupt and incompetent. Many, for example, exaggerated the number of men under their command, in order to receive more pay. Throughout the whole struggle with the North, the army had shown a consistent reluctance to do any fighting. Most were quite happy to let the Americans fight the communists for them.

Perhaps worst of all was the desertion rate. During the course of any one year, one in ten South Vietnamese soldiers would desert. Vietnamization only increased this problem. Sometimes deserters would hide their uniforms and pretend to be Vietcong guerrillas who

RESENTFUL TROOPS

Vietnamization stirred up further resentment among American troops, even though it was intended to take pressure off them. American private Thomas Kingsley wrote to a friend: *"…there's a bitter hatred between us and the South Viet Nam troops because they carry new weapons and we don't; and we do all the goddamn fighting while they sit on their asses all the time. Man, it makes you burn."*

"Anyone who isn't confused doesn't really understand the situation."

ED MURROW, AMERICAN JOURNALIST, 1969

were surrendering to the South under the 'Open arms' policy of the time, which offered money and other incentives to rebels if they gave themselves up.

TROOPS RETURN

But Nixon did have some successes. The troop withdrawals he ordered had a noticeable impact on the anti-war protests. As soldiers came home, the demonstrations became less well attended, although they still went on. Nixon and his Vice-president Spiro Agnew also launched ferocious attacks on their opponents at home. Playing up the fact that many demonstrators were middle-class students, and some of the war's most vociferous supporters were working class, Agnew called them "an effete corp of impudent snobs".

▼ Summoning as much pomp and ceremony as their weary faces can muster, US troops march out of their base at Quang Tri on the first step of their return home. US troop numbers in Vietnam declined rapidly after Nixon came to power.

US STILL OPTIMISTIC OF VICTORY

Like the Johnson and Kennedy governments before them, Nixon and Kissinger believed America's great wealth, military power and technological superiority could win them the war. During the summer of 1969, America achieved the astounding feat of placing men on the Moon. If they could do that, surely they could beat a tiny little country in Southeast Asia?

THE MY LAI MASSACRE

In early 1969, as the shock waves from Tet died away, a much smaller incident took place which was to have a similarly profound effect on public perceptions of the war. On 16th March, a number of American soldiers under the command of Lieutenant William Calley, rounded up around 500 men, women and children of the village of My Lai, lined them up in a ditch, and murdered them.

Massacres like My Lai were not everyday occurrences in Vietnam, but neither were they one-off events. My Lai came to symbolise the attitude of many US soldiers to the Vietnamese they were supposed to be protecting. Historian Loren Baritz evoked an image of "nineteen-year-old Americans, brought up on World War II movies and Westerns, walking through the jungle, armed to the teeth, searching for an invisible enemy…". Many of these young men found the

▶ Even the presence of a press photographer did not prevent this American soldier punching a captured and disarmed Vietcong guerrilla. Such violence was often prompted by the frustration American soldiers felt being attacked by an invisible enemy who could strike at any time and then vanish into the jungle.

As a 'med evac' (medical evacuation) helicopter hovers in the background, American troops sift through the grisly remains of a Vietcong ambush. Communist troops favoured such hit and run tactics, which allowed them to attack the Americans only when they felt the situation was to their advantage.

peasant lifestyle and Buddhist customs of the rural Vietnamese baffling. They spoke of them as 'dinks', 'slopes', 'gooks', or in similar racist terms.

As members of their platoon were picked off one by one in booby traps, sniper fire or hit-and-run ambushes, by an enemy they almost never saw, many American soldiers came to regard all Vietnamese as 'the enemy'.

When the facts about My Lai emerged a year or so later, it was not just anti-war protesters who were outraged. Many Americans who supported the war were shocked to hear of their own army behaving with the same callous brutality as the Imperial Japanese or Nazi troops of the Second World War.

A GI'S BITTERNESS

This is a war of the Unwilling
Led by the Unqualified
Dying for the Ungrateful

GRAFFITI IN GI LAVATORY, SAIGON

41

CHAPTER SEVEN

The war spreads 1970-1973

CAMBODIA AND LAOS DRAWN IN

Vietnam shares its western border with two countries – Cambodia and Laos. Now both would be drawn into the conflict. In Cambodia the anti-communist government of Prince Sihanouk had opposed US involvement in the Vietnam war, and had even cut diplomatic relations with America because of it. Sihanouk had an understanding with the North Vietnamese that he would permit the Ho Chi Minh trail to pass through his country if they did not support the Cambodian communist guerrillas – the Khmer Rouge. This understanding worked well until both the Vietnamese forces in Cambodia, and the Khmer Rouge, became too strong to ignore.

Sihanouk memorably described his country as being "caught between the hammer and the anvil". In March 1970 he was ousted from power and replaced by Lon Nol, a pro-American general who disapproved of Sihanouk's understanding with the North Vietnamese.

INVASION OF CAMBODIA

One of Nixon's first decisions in the Vietnam War had been to bomb North Vietnamese bases in Cambodia. Now, with a pro-American regime in control of the country, he authorized an out-and-out ground attack. On 30th April 1970, 80,000 South Vietnamese and American troops poured over the border to seek out and destroy North Vietnamese bases.

▼ Vietnam, Laos and Cambodia had been united in one French colony – Indochina. The Mekong River linked them all, and each was cloaked in thick tropical vegetation.

Indochina 1908 - 1954

Their main target was the Central Office for South Vietnam (COSVN) – the North's military headquarters in Cambodia. But when they got there they found a few deserted huts. The military planners, and the forces they commanded, had vanished into the jungle. No sooner had the Americans and South Vietnamese left than they came back. Once again, North Vietnam's low-technology approach to the war had paid off.

The invasion had catastrophic consequences for Cambodia. The North Vietnamese began to aid the Khmer Rouge, who they had previously ignored. Fighting between the Khmer Rouge and Lon Nol's government escalated into full-scale civil war and led to an eventual communist victory.

The spin-off for Nixon and America was minor in comparison. Many Americans were deeply unhappy about this extension of a war which was supposed to be coming to an end. During demonstrations six students were shot dead at Kent State University, Ohio, and Jackson, Mississippi, by American military forces fearful that these protests would turn into riots.

▲ This picture appeared on newspaper front pages throughout the world. It shows the anguish of one student demonstrator at Kent State University, Ohio, as she surveys the body of one of the students shot dead during anti-war protests there.

LAOS IN THE FIRING LINE

In Laos similar circumstances provoked another invasion nine months later. On 30th January, 1971, South Vietnamese troops, heavily supported by American aircraft and artillery positions, attacked North Vietnamese forces there. Although the planes and artillery inflicted losses, the South Vietnamese troops fought badly against their Northern counterparts. After the initial attack they fled in chaos.

▲ President Nixon during his historic visit to China in 1972. He poses for press photographers on the Great Wall with Chinese Premier Zhou En Lai.

DÉTENTE?

All this was heartening news for the North Vietnamese commanders. Since 1968 they had been rebuilding their forces for another great offensive. But as the 70s wore on, they felt that time was running out. The North's policy of hanging on grimly had kept them going against the immensely powerful Americans, but the awful grind of the war was taking its toll on the North's supporters. During the early 1970s the talk in world politics was of détente – a French word meaning 'relaxation'. After two decades of outright hostility, the leaders of America, China and the Soviet Union had all concluded that the world would be a safer place if relations between them improved. To move the process on, President Nixon visited both countries, and for most of the decade the Cold War became a little less frosty.

For the leaders of both North and South Vietnam this was not good news. Both had been sustained and owed their survival to the rival superpowers of the Cold War. As the conflict dragged on, both sensed their powerful friends were losing interest.

THE EASTER OFFENSIVE

The North Vietnamese attack began on 30th March 1972. It was to become known as the Easter Offensive. Guerrillas in the South rose up, and Northern troops swarmed over the Demilitarized Zone and out from their bases in Cambodia and into the South. Their strategy assumed that Southern troops would melt before them, as they had done in Laos. At first this seemed to be the case, and the offensive went extremely well.

Like the South Vietnamese, American forces were caught by surprise. But, as before, when faced with a straightforward battle they reacted extremely effectively. Nixon immediately authorized massive air attacks against military targets in the North. American Navy ships off the coast of Vietnam blockaded the country, and mines were placed in the main Northern harbour of Haiphong. Then, the South Vietnamese army launched a massive and successful counter-attack, with US air and artillery support.

The offensive was a disaster for the North. They lost 100,000 men, and still President Thieu was in power in Saigon. He, in turn, had lost only 25,000 of his men in this latest attack – a quarter of the Northern casualties. Furthermore, although their Chinese and Soviet allies had made strong public protests against the American bombing, in private they were still urging the North to negotiate with America and bring the war to an end.

PARIS PEACE TALKS

So it was that the Paris Peace Talks, which had dragged on since May 1968, eventually began to bear fruit. In October 1972 Henry Kissinger, and the North's principal negotiator Le Duc Tho, announced they had reached an agreement that would be acceptable to them both.

But Kissinger had not consulted the South Vietnamese to reach this settlement. Although they took part in the Paris Peace Talks, they had no interest in America withdrawing from the war. Their lack of cooperation had hindered the talks considerably. When Kissinger brought the agreement to Thieu he rejected it angrily. The North Vietnamese in turn were very suspicious of this. They saw Thieu's refusal as a ploy, and the talks foundered.

THE PARIS AGREEMENT

The main points agreed between Henry Kissinger and Le Duc Tho were:

- There would be an immediate cease-fire.

- The armies would keep control of whatever territory they held at the time of the cease-fire.

- American troops would leave the country within 60 days.

- Prisoners of war would be exchanged.

- A political settlement would be negotiated after the cease-fire. This would include democratic elections and the reunification of Vietnam.

PEACE BREAKS DOWN

In December of 1972 Nixon ordered further, massive air strikes against North Vietnam. These were to be the most intense bombing attacks of the war. They went on for eleven days, and caused a huge outcry, not only from America's traditional enemies, and anti-war protesters, but also from America's European allies.

The attacks were partially carried out to encourage the North to make more concessions at the peace talks, but also to reassure Thieu that America was not deserting the South. Massive military aid followed too, to strengthen the South Vietnamese army.

▶ Facing each other with steely, poker-faced determination, American and North Vietnamese diplomats negotiate at the Paris Peace Talks. In the centre of each picture are Henry Kissinger (above) and Le Duc Tho (below).

PEACE WITH HONOUR?

The talks began again in January. Following American threats to sign a treaty without the South, Thieu reluctantly agreed to a set of conditions very similar to those announced by Kissinger and Le Duc Tho in October 1972. On 27th January America and North and South Vietnam signed the 'Paris Agreement'. True to the agreement the last American combat soldier left South Vietnam on 29th March 1973.

Nixon announced the breakthrough by saying "We have finally achieved peace with honour". But he and the rest of his government knew this was a sham. Despite the billions of dollars and thousands of lives the United States had sacrificed in Vietnam, the regime they had supported so strongly was still no more capable of defending itself against its communist opponents than it had been in 1963.

AMERICAN MORALE

Even in the early 1970s, many Western policy makers still saw America's war against communism in Vietnam, as immensely important.

"The future of Western civilisation is at stake in the way you handle yourselves in Vietnam."

SIR ROBERT THOMPSON, BRITISH GUERRILLA WARFARE SPECIALIST, TO RICHARD NIXON. 1971

But at the same time, many American soldiers felt they were fighting a war they neither believed in, nor hoped they could win, and the morale of America's troops in Vietnam plummeted alarmingly. Black and Latino soldiers especially felt that they had been singled out to do the worst of the fighting. Some soldiers began to paint peace signs and anti-war slogans on their uniforms. Officers would have to argue with men who refused to obey orders during combat. Drug taking increased to the point where it became commonplace. Unpopular officers were sometimes killed by their own men, often by a fragmentation grenade rolled into their tent at night – a practice known as 'fragging'.

"No Vietcong ever called me nigger."

BLACK GI SLOGAN

"The frank thing is, there just wasn't a hell of a lot worth dying for."

LIEUTENANT BILL KENERLY

◀ Many American soldiers in Vietnam made no secret of their opposition to the war. These troops are giving the 'V' peace sign, popularized by such anti-war celebrities as John Lennon. A 'ban the bomb' flag also flies over their position.

CHAPTER EIGHT

The final conflict 1973-1975

A FRAGILE PEACE

With America gone, South Vietnam held out for two years, one month and a day. Perhaps it is surprising that they lasted as long as that.

No one seriously expected the Paris Agreement to end the war. When the cease-fire was declared, North and South Vietnam were as far apart as ever. Many expected a Northern victory sooner, but the defeat of South Vietnam was not as certain as it might appear.

The North used the 1973 cease-fire to buy time, and recover from the devastating losses of the Easter Offensive. In June of that year the North Vietnamese leader Le Duan visited both his communist allies, China and the Soviet Union. He hoped to persuade them to supply more aid for a final offensive. But neither of the two communist superpowers showed much interest. In the era of détente, both were far more concerned with improving relations with the United States.

▼ As the war wound down US prisoners of war were freed. Almost all of them were captured pilots or other aircrew. These Americans were photographed in Hanoi in March 1973, as they began their journey home.

Although it was ironic that both sides of the Vietnam war lost the full-scale support of their superpower backers at the same time, this had far less effect on the North. After all, no Chinese or Soviet troops had fought in Vietnam.

In the South, the Americans left behind a detachment of 159 marines to guard their embassy. Another 10,000 American civilians remained too, most of whom had close connections with the military. They also left billions of dollars worth of military bases and equipment in the South. After Paris, Nixon promised President Thieu he was not deserting him, and threatened the North with dire consequences should they break the cease-fire. With an army that was now a million men strong, and equipped with the best military technology available, the South Vietnamese did indeed look like they had a fighting chance.

A NORTH VIETNAMESE PERSPECTIVE

"Our troops were exhausted and their units in disarray. We had not been able to make up our losses. We were short of manpower as well as food and ammunition, and coping with the enemy was very difficult."

NORTH VIETNAMESE GENERAL TRAN VAN TRA ON THE CONDITION OF HIS MEN FIGHTING IN THE SOUTH IN 1973

AT WAR AGAIN

The cease-fire soon broke down. At first, the South Vietnamese army performed surprisingly well. No doubt the knowledge that they were really on their own now spurred them on. Much of the territory lost to the North before the Paris Agreement was recovered. But the North held on. While they regained their strength, they reverted to low-key guerrilla tactics, and waited. They could afford to bide their time. In 1973 they were the third biggest army in the world, and were armed with some of the best equipment available.

Despite all its advantages, Thieu's government was still doomed. America had hoped its billions of dollars and 500,000 troops would enable South Vietnam to establish itself as a strong and viable nation. But it had never been able to do this. The government in Saigon had never managed to gain any widespread support from the mainly peasant, Buddhist population of South Vietnam. Thieu's main allies were the armed forces, but even they were divided in their support.

AN ARMY IN DISARRAY

South Vietnam's fighting forces were also hopelessly corrupt. They were led by commanders who paid their soldiers so little they had to steal food to survive. American officers had the comfort of knowing that if their troops were pinned down by the enemy, they could radio for air support. Within minutes, American jets would scream over the horizon and rain down bullets and missiles on their opponents. South Vietnamese soldiers had to bribe their airforce to fly missions to support them.

Worse was to come. American aid still continued, but the sophisticated weapons they left behind needed fuel and spare parts that the South Vietnamese could neither obtain nor afford. The country's economy, already reeling from the loss of 300,000 jobs provided by the American presence, also suffered from both a poor rice harvest and a global fuel crisis brought on by massive increases in the price of oil.

THE WORLD TURNS ITS BACK

By October 1973, barely nine months after the cease-fire was declared, full-scale war was raging in Vietnam. But no one in the rest of the world was particularly interested. Most of the world's war correspondents and photographers were engrossed in the Middle East, where another major American ally, Israel, was fighting for survival against its hostile Arab neighbours.

Nixon, too, was sinking fast, his presidency fatally tarnished by the Watergate scandal. (A series of dirty tricks Nixon's Republican Party played on their Democrat rivals in the 1972 presidential election.) He resigned in August 1974, to

---

CASUALTY FIGURES

These are the final casualty figures for the Second Indochina War, covering the period from 1954 to 1975. Although their accuracy cannot be guaranteed, they are broadly accepted by historians.

NORTH VIETNAM

1,100,000 soldiers killed

600,000 soldiers wounded

26,000 soldiers captured

2,000,000 civilians killed

SOUTH VIETNAM

223,748 soldiers killed

1,169,763 soldiers wounded

415,000 civilians killed

UNITED STATES

47,378 soldiers killed

304,704 soldiers wounded

766 soldiers captured

be replaced by his Vice-president Gerald Ford. Although Ford reassured the South Vietnamese he would continue to support them, neither he nor his government had any good reason to do so.

NORTH VIETNAM'S LAST OFFENSIVE

By the end of 1974, the North felt strong enough to attempt another offensive. As ever, they hoped that an attack on the South would trigger an uprising against Thieu's regime. Whatever they did though, they decided to do cautiously. Still unsure of America's intentions, they feared their former enemy may react with a massive bombing campaign.

In December 1974, North Vietnamese forces attacked and quickly overran the central highlands province of Phuoc Long. But America did not react, and further attacks in early 1975 brought further advances. Thieu ordered his army to retreat and form a defensive line just north of Saigon. The retreat turned into a chaotic rout. Sensing that defeat was inevitable, thousands deserted and half a million refugees poured into Saigon. Thieu resigned on 21st April. In his farewell speech he promised to "stand shoulder to shoulder with the compatriots and combatants to defend the country…" but instead he fled to Taiwan.

▼ South Vietnamese refugees, desperate to flee from the approaching Northern forces, board a cargo ship at Da Nang in 1975.

▲ Fear of execution by communist soldiers made escape a matter of life or death for many South Vietnamese. Here at Nha Trang in April 1975, an American official punches a man away from an aeroplane already dangerously overloaded with refugees.

THE LAST BATTLE

North Vietnamese novelist Duong Thu Huong describes the final battle for Saigon in her book *Novel Without a Name*:

"The battle unfolded as predictably as if it had been a parade: assault, a rapid conclusion. Compared to the battles of the last ten years, it almost seemed like a game…"

SAIGON FALLS

North Vietnamese troops reached Saigon so quickly that the United States had to airlift 900 of its own men, and 5,000 Vietnamese, out of the capital to aircraft carriers waiting off the coast. TV news showed unforgettable shots of terrified Vietnamese officials, certain that they would be executed if they stayed behind, fighting desperately to gain a place aboard an evacuation helicopter. Out at sea, aircraft carrier flightdecks became so crowded empty helicopters were pushed into the water to make way for incoming craft. This final terrible waste of expensive technology seemed a fitting symbol of America's involvement in the war. These ships were also besieged by South Vietnamese fleeing by boat. One aircraft carrier took on an extraordinary 10,000 refugees.

In Saigon, TV crews filmed a North Vietnamese T-54 tank battering down the iron railings of the presidential palace. Others followed behind. Bounding from the leading tank was Colonel Bui Tin, who entered the palace to take the South Vietnamese surrender.

Waiting for him was Thieu's replacement, General Duang Van Minh. He greeted Bui Tin with these words: "I have been waiting since early this morning to transfer power to you." Bui Tin was brusque and brutally honest. "There's no question of you transferring power. Your power has crumbled. You cannot give up what you do not have."

The city fell with little fighting. After thirty years and over three million deaths, the Vietnam War had finally ground to a halt.

▼ A North Vietnamese tank crashes through the railings of Saigon's presidential palace on 30th of April, 1975. The fall of Saigon marked the end of thirty years of fighting.

CHAPTER NINE

The consequences of the war 1976 to the present

LE DUAN'S TRIUMPH

On 15th May, 1975, Vietnamese leader Le Duan delivered these triumphal words during celebrations in Hanoi to mark the communist victory: "We hail the new era... of brilliant prospects for the development of a peaceful, independent, reunified, democratic, prosperous and strong Vietnam..."

But, even today, those brilliant prospects are yet to come. The story of Vietnam in peace is almost as tragic as Vietnam at war.

RE-EDUCATION

When the North Vietnamese arrived in Saigon many government and military officials who had not managed to escape, feared for their lives. After all, government representatives had been killed in their thousands in the city of Hue, when it was occupied by the North during the Tet Offensive. But the expected massacre did not take place. Instead, South Vietnamese officials were sent to re-education camps – where they were force-fed communist teachings and asked to repent their former lives. It was unpleasant and sinister, but it could have been much worse.

▼ This famous photograph shows American and South Vietnamese officials on the roof of the US Embassy in Saigon, just before the city fell. They await a fleet of helicopters to ferry them to US aircraft carriers and safety.

THE DOMINOES FALL

Much worse happened to Vietnam's neighbours. Here, the 'domino theory' became a self-fulfilling prophecy. American intervention in Laos and Cambodia led directly to increased communist opposition. As the Vietnam War ended, both its neighbours were also taken over by communist regimes. In Laos the Pathet Lao party murdered 100,000 of its pro-American Hmong guerrilla opponents.

YEAR ZERO IN CAMBODIA

When they took over Cambodia, the Khmer Rouge called for a complete social revolution. They declared 1975 to be 'Year Zero' and set about systematically eliminating anyone they suspected of being 'bourgeois' (middle class). To this grotesque and fanatical regime, even owning a pair of glasses, or having soft hands, was evidence enough to warrant execution. At least a million Cambodians died in what became known as 'the killing fields', before the regime fell in December 1978.

CHAOS IN CAMBODIA

In Cambodia far worse happened. The Khmer Rouge captured the capital Phnom Penh on 17th of April – two weeks before Saigon fell to the North. Led by a despotic communist named Pol Pot, the Khmer Rouge emptied Cambodia's cities and forced their inhabitants to work in agricultural communes. Eventually, after nearly four years, a Vietnamese invasion deposed this ugly regime.

▼ These piles of skulls at a Cambodian village are grisly reminders of the terrible atrocities inflicted on Cambodia by the Khmer Rouge.

Vietnam's intervention, in December 1978, was brought about in part by border conflicts with the Khmer Rouge. But it provoked a brief invasion of North Vietnam by their former ally China, who supported the Khmers. This is turn led to the ugly persecution in Vietnam of Vietnamese of Chinese origin.

THE LEGACY OF WAR

Physically, Vietnam was left in an appalling state by the war. The bombing had left huge craters over much of the country, and destroyed a great deal of its industry and transport system. Defoliant chemicals sprayed by American planes had polluted and destroyed much of its fertile land. Peasants too, had been driven from their fields for much of the war, and many were reluctant to return. The result was near starvation. Mines, and unexploded bombs and shells, also littered the country. Many of the victims of these remnants from the war would be women and children.

America had spent $167 billion on Vietnam while it was at war. China and the Soviet Union had also spent undisclosed but vast amounts of money of their own. Now the war was over, the world superpowers had little left to give. Once she had fallen out with the Chinese over Cambodia, Vietnam had only the Soviet Union as a friend. Unfortunately, in the late 70s and early 80s, the Soviets had little money to spare for their allies, as their own economy was in such a poor state.

▼ This photograph, taken in 1972, shows the devastated city of Quang Tri. Vietnam would take many decades to recover from the destruction brought by the war.

THE BOAT PEOPLE

Vietnam became one of the poorest countries in the world. As problems mounted, many people decided to flee the country. If they paid the government a fee they were allowed to leave on dangerously overcrowded boats, and cast at the mercy of storms, pirates, and any foreign government that would have them. Over 1.5 million 'boat people' chose to go, and most ended up in refugee camps in Hong Kong, Thailand and Malaysia. The episode was a deeply shameful one for Vietnam, and many refugees were sent back home, by neighbouring countries unable to cope with such a huge influx. One million though, did manage to emigrate to the United States – another consequence of the war.

▲ Vietnamese "boat people", stranded in the Philippines for 10 weeks in 1979, beg passing ships for water.

CHILDREN OF THE DUST

Just as tragic were the thousands of children born to Vietnamese women and American servicemen. Most were either unknown to, or abandoned by, their American fathers. In post-war Vietnam, they were called 'children of the dust', and so despised and rejected by their fellow citizens that most had to beg to stay alive.

VIETNAM 'VETS'

In America, veterans often faced a chilly reception. Shunned and ashamed, many turned to drugs and alcohol to try to wipe out their nightmare stay in Vietnam. Divorce, unemployment and crime rates among Vietnam veterans are all noticeably higher than those of their generation who did not go to fight.

CHANGE BEYOND RECOGNITION

American soldiers called their homeland 'the World'. But when they got back there, many found things bewilderingly different.

"I didn't come home; I just came back. Home had changed so much that I didn't recognize it. And no one recognized me either."

ANONYMOUS G.I., QUOTED IN JOHN CLARK PRATT'S "VIETNAM VOICES"

"I managed to survive Vietnam and got back to New York… The change was just shocking. Clothes had changed. People's attitudes had changed. Close friends… that had been clean-cut, athletic types… now had hair down to their shoulders. They were wearin'… beards and bell bottom pants… an' givin' peace signs. And I think I, like a lot of other guys, just kind of withdrew."

CORPORAL VITO J. LAVACCA

DISILLUSIONMENT

On a grander scale, the way that the American Government had consistently lied about its actions in Vietnam, and hidden the truth of what was happening in that country from its people, led to a widespread disenchantment and loss of respect for authority in the United States. The street demonstrations that had provoked such violent clashes between police and protesters were a symptom of this. Black soldiers, especially, felt they had had to bear the brunt of much of the fighting. This too contributed to an increased feeling of alienation between many blacks and the essentially white elite that ran the country. Even the churches in America were divided over their support for the war. (Generally, the more fundamentalist branches of Christianity supported the war, and the more liberal churches did not.)

Vietnam shaped American foreign policy for the rest of the century. The American Government and people had lost faith in the technological superiority of their armed forces. Other potential Vietnams, such as communist uprisings in Nicaragua and El Salvador in Central America, were dealt with more cunningly. (America secretly funded or trained the anti-communist opposition, and had no direct involvement.) Only when they could be 100% sure of a knockout victory were American troops committed to battle. (US soldiers invaded Grenada in 1983, for example, when the tiny Caribbean island was taken over by a Marxist regime.)

DIFFERING VIEWS

Over the decades, American historians have agonized over why their intervention in Vietnam was such a disaster. Some historians support the view of General Westmoreland, who believed that the United States lost the war because the civilian government, influenced by the anti-

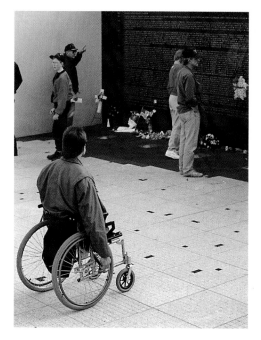

▼ US soldiers returned home to find their own sacrifices were largely unappreciated. But in the years since the war, memorials have been built to commemorate the men who died. Here a legless veteran of the war visits a memorial in St Paul, Minnesota.

war protesters and an unsympathetic media, held back the armed forces. Westmoreland believed he could have won if he had been allowed to make full use of America's military might and wage a full-scale conflict.

Others see this view as too simplistic. They believe the war was unwinnable because the South Vietnamese regime the United States supported was too unstable. They feel that America relied too much on its technological superiority, and understood too little of the unique situation of Vietnam.

OPPOSING ATTITUDES

Two quotes sum up the attitude of the North Vietnamese and Americans, and explain why one won and the other lost:

"If we must fight, we will fight. You can kill ten of my men for every one I kill of yours. But even at those odds, you will lose and I will win."

HO CHI MINH IN 1946, TO THE FRENCH PRIME MINISTER, AT THE START OF THE CONFLICT

"I can't believe that a fourth-rate power like North Vietnam doesn't have a breaking point."

HENRY KISSINGER, 1969, WHILST TRYING TO FORCE THE VIETNAMESE TO MAKE CONCESSIONS AT THE PARIS PEACE TALKS

PEACE IN VIETNAM

Today Vietnam is still a very poor country, but peace has settled on the land. America eventually recognized the new government in 1995 and since then Vietnam has been building better relations with Western nations. Communist economic policies, such as collectivized farming have been dropped, and private enterprise is now encouraged. Tourism is a major money earner. Along with the beautiful temples and lush scenery, visitors also come to see crashed bombers, left where they fell, burned-out tanks, and other ruins of the war.

THE UNWINNABLE WAR

In the 1960s Vice-president Hubert Humphrey had privately said of Vietnam: "America is throwing lives and money down a corrupt rat hole." It was all too true. But his own President, Lyndon Johnson, had also said: "The battle against communism must be joined in Southeast Asia with strength and determination… or the United States, inevitably, must surrender the Pacific and take up our defenses on our own shores." Johnson and America's belief that this was the case led them into an unwinnable war which would have terrible consequences for both America and Vietnam.

Timeline

1861
French forces seize Saigon and the French take substantial control of Vietnam

1883
France rules 'Indochina' (present-day Laos, Cambodia and Vietnam) as a single colony

1890
Ho Chi Minh born (He leaves Vietnam in 1911)

1924
Ho becomes full time communist agent for Soviet Union

1949
Communists seize control of China

1950
JUNE
Korean War begins. US provides military aid for French in Vietnam

1954
MAY
French surrender at Dien Bien Phu
JULY
Geneva Conference followed by Geneva Accords peace settlement.

Vietnam temporarily divided into communist North and non-communist South

DECEMBER
North Vietnam sends its first regular troops to fight in the South

1964
Gulf of Tonkin Resolution gives US president the power to engage US combat troops in Vietnam without a formal declaration of war

1965
FEBRUARY
US tactical air strikes and strategic bombing begin in Vietnam
MARCH
First US combat troops arrive in Vietnam

JULY
President Johnson commits the US to a full scale war in Vietnam

JUNE
US troop withdrawal begins in Vietnam
SEPTEMBER
Ho Chi Minh dies

1970
War spreads to Cambodia

1971
War spreads to Laos

1972
FEBRUARY
Nixon visits China
MARCH/APRIL
North Vietnamese Easter Offensive
MAY
Nixon visits Soviet Union

1940

Japan occupies Indochina, but French colonial administration continues to control the colony

1941

Ho returns to Vietnam and forms Vietminh to fight against Japan and France

1945

Ho declares independence of Vietnam, but French continue to control country

1946

NOVEMBER
French warships bombard Haiphong
DECEMBER
Vietminh forces begin drawn out war against French

1955

Ngo Dinh Diem elected president of South Vietnam

1957

Civil War breaks out in South Vietnam between government troops and communist guerrillas

1962

US establishes military forces in South Vietnam

1963

NOVEMBER
US President John F. Kennedy assassinated. Diem assassinated. A succession of South Vietnamese leaders follow

1967

SEPTEMBER
Nguyen Van Thieu elected president of South Vietnam

OCTOBER
Major demonstrations across the US against America's involvement in the Vietnam War

1968

JANUARY
Tet Offensive
MARCH
My Lai massacre
MAY
Paris peace negotiations begin

1969

Nixon replaces Johnson as US president

1973

JANUARY
'Paris Peace Agreement' allows US to withdraw from Vietnam
MARCH
Last US troops leave Vietnam

1974

South Vietnam launches offensive against communist guerrillas in the South

1975

JANUARY
North Vietnam begins final offensive which will result in victory over the South

APRIL
Khmer Rouge take control of Cambodia. Saigon falls to communist forces and Vietnam War is over

Glossary

ARVN Army of the Republic of Vietnam. South Vietnam's main fighting force.

assassination The deliberate killing of a political leader, in order to bring about political change.

capitalism A type of economic system where factories and other businesses, and property, is owned by individuals rather than the state.

Cold War A period after the Second World War lasting from 1945 to 1991 when the Soviet Union (now Russia) and its allies, and the United States and its allies, were very hostile and mistrustful of each other.

colony A territory occupied by a country in order to exploit its wealth.

commando A special soldier trained for dangerous hit and run raids, usually behind enemy lines.

communism A type of economic system where the state owns factories, other businesses, and property.

conspiracy A secret plan.

containment American policy which sought to 'contain' communism in one country and stop it 'spreading' to another. (See 'domino theory'.)

corruption In this sense, a situation where government officials steal money in taxes and foreign aid for themselves, rather than spend it on their country.

deserter A member of the armed forces who flees from fighting.

détente A diplomatic term meaning a 'lessening of tension' between former enemies, leading to a period of greater understanding between them.

DMZ Demilitarized Zone – in Vietnam, a stretch of land that separated North Vietnam from South Vietnam.

domino theory The idea that if one country 'fell' to communism, then all the other countries around it would also 'fall' – like a row of stacked-up dominoes.

guerrilla A member of an informal armed force, usually fighting a stronger regular army by hit-and-run tactics.

herbicide A chemical that kills plants.

napalm A jelly-like chemical that bursts into flames on contact with air.

offensive In this sense, a full scale attack by an army.

pacification In this sense, a campaign to stamp out communist guerrilla activity in South Vietnam.

Pyrric victory A victory that is as costly as a defeat.

regime A system of government, or a particular group of people in government.

stalemate A situation where neither side in a conflict can win.

technology The practical application of scientific discoveries to the manufacture of machines.

Vietcong or VC A term used by the Southern Vietnamese and Americans to describe the communist guerrillas who fought in South Vietnam.

Vietminh A term used to describe the broad group of parties who supported Ho Chi Minh in North Vietnam.

Vietnamization An American policy aimed at phasing out American combat troops in Vietnam, and replacing them with equally effective South Vietnamese combat troops.

Further Information

BOOKS

Mitchell Hall *The Vietnam War* (Longman, 2000) A thorough account of the war, written with great clarity and with additional historic source material.

Stanley Karnow *Vietnam* (Viking Press, 1983) Fascinating, highly-readable account by a journalist with first-hand experience of the war and its leading personalities.

John Clark Pratt *Vietnam Voices* (Penguin, 1984) Otto J. Lehrack *No Shining Armor – The Marines at War in Vietnam.* (University Press of Kansas, 1992) Two fascinating compendiums of reminiscences by American soldiers who fought in the war.

Time-Life *The Vietnam Experience* (Time Life, 1981) Sprawling, carefully researched and exhaustively illustrated.

Duong Thu Huong *Novel Without a Name* (Morrow/Avon, 1995) Written as a novel, this is a poignant account of the fighting from a Northern perspective.

Neil Sheehan *A Bright and Shining Lie* (Vintage Books, 1989) Riveting account of American soldier John Paul Vann's time in Vietnam until his death in a helicopter accident in 1972.

Michael Herr *Dispatches* (Picador, 1997) On-the-spot reminiscences, written in sizzling '60s hipspeak, by one of the screen writers of "Apocalypse Now".

Tim O'Brien *If I Die in a Combat Zone* (Flamingo, 1989) First-hand account of his tour of duty by a Vietnamese veteran.

FILMS

Although as near to fact as any other Hollywood film, the following movies all give a taste of the sights and sounds of America's war in Vietnam.

The Deer Hunter (1978)
Apocalypse Now (1979)
Platoon (1986)
Full Metal Jacket (1987)
Casualties of War (1988)
Born on the Fourth of July (1989)

WEBSITES

A small selection of sites worth visiting:

http://www.pbs.org/wgbh/amex/vietnam/
Good quality site set up by the American Public Broadcast Service, with transcripts from their TV series *Vietnam The American Experience*

http://web20.paralynx.com/vets/hisintro.html
A history of the Vietnam War set up by the 'Vets With A Mission' organisation, a group of Vietnam veterans and non-veterans who are dedicated "to bringing healing, reconciliation and renewal to the people of Vietnam".

http://members.aol.com/veterans/warlib6v.htm
Exhaustive links and resources library set up by the American War Library.

http://servercc.oakton.edu/~wittman/
Calling itself 'Vietnam Yesterday and Today' this is a typical small, college-based website.

Visit www.learn.co.uk for more resources

Index